D1537620

Biggest Machines

Library of Congress Number: 80-383

2 3 4 5 6 7 8 9 0 84 83 82 81 80

Printed in the United States of America.

Library of Congress Cataloging in Publication Data

Kiley, Denise, 1948-
  Biggest machines.

  Includes index.
  SUMMARY: Describes some of the largest
machines in the world and the tasks they perform.
  1. Machinery—Juvenile literature.
[1. Machinery] I. Title.
TJ147.K54 621.8 80-383
ISBN 0-8172-1332-5 lib. bdg.

Photographs appear through the courtesy of the following:
Air Portraits (U.K.): pp. 28-29
Allen-Bradley: pp. 10-11
Balderson: pp. 6-7
Boeing Commercial Airplane Company: pp. 22-23
British Hovercraft Corp. (U.K.): pp. 14-15
Bucyrus-Eris: cover, pp. 4-5
Cunard: pp. 12-13
Department of the Air Force: pp. 24-25
National Motor Museum (U.K.): pp. 20-21
Terex: pp. 8-9
United Press International Photo: pp. 26-27
U.S. Naval Photographic Center: pp. 16-17, 18-19
WABCO Construction and Mining Equipment Group: p. 3

biggest
MACHINES

Denise Kiley

RAINTREE CHILDRENS BOOKS
Milwaukee • Toronto • Melbourne • London

Machines, Machines, Machines. They are everywhere in our lives. In this book you will find out about some of the biggest machines in the world.

This is the Big Muskie. It is an earth-moving machine called a

dragline. It is used to dig very large holes. In one scoop, the bucket can dig up enough earth to fill more than 25 dump trucks. The Big Muskie weighs about as much as 10,000 cars.

This earth-moving machine is called the Double Dude. The huge blade is about 48 feet (15 meters) long and 6 feet (2 meters) high. It weighs more than 27,000 pounds (12,247 kilograms).

The Double Dude is used to push dirt into holes to fill them up. If there were a hole twelve feet deep, six feet wide, and one mile long, the Double Dude could fill it with earth in about one hour.

Here is the Titan. It is the biggest dump truck in the world. It is so big that it cannot travel on streets or highways. The Titan must be sent in several parts to where it will be used. The parts are then put together.

The Titan can hold 700,000 pounds (317,515 kilograms) of earth. One of its tires weighs as much as three cars.

The world's largest four-faced clock is in Milwaukee, Wisconsin. Actually, there are four separate clocks in the tower. The face is

more than 40 feet (12 meters) across. The minute hand is 20 feet (6 meters) long. The clock weighs about 50 tons.

The first passenger ship sailed across the Atlantic Ocean almost 150 years ago. The newest, and largest, passenger ship is the Queen Elizabeth 2. It made its first voyage in 1969.

The Queen Elizabeth 2 has a 1,000-person crew. It can carry almost 2,000 passengers.

The Queen Elizabeth 2 is almost like a floating city. It has a

hospital, restaurants, stores, libraries, a bank, theaters, and sports facilities.

The ship is 963 feet (293.5 meters) long. It weighs over 67,000 tons. It takes five days to sail across the Atlantic Ocean. Because of the cost of traveling on the Queen Elizabeth 2, it will probably be the last ocean liner ever built.

This vehicle is a hovercraft. It is also called an ACV — <u>a</u>ir-<u>c</u>ushion <u>v</u>ehicle. Large engines blow air out the bottom of the craft. There is so much air pressure that the craft lifts above the ground, or water. Propeller engines on the deck push the hovercraft forward on the air cushion.

Hovercraft can carry people and cars across water. This SRN-4 is the largest hovercraft. It can carry 30 cars and several hundred passengers. The SRN-4 can go about 70 miles per hour (113 kilometers per hour).

This warship is the U.S.S. Nimitz. Along with the U.S.S. Dwight D. Eisenhower, it is the largest aircraft carrier. It is 1,092 feet (332.8 meters) long. More than 90 airplanes can take off and land on the deck.

The ship has nuclear-powered engines. It can travel about 900,000 miles (1,448,000 kilometers) without refueling. It needs 6,300 people to run the ship. It costs about $2 billion to build the ship.

The largest battleships ever built were the Japanese ships Yamato and Musashi. They were both sunk during World War II.

The largest battleship today is the one on this page, the U.S.S.

New Jersey. The New Jersey was in
World War II, the Korean War and
the war in Vietnam. The New
Jersey went out of active service
in 1969.

The largest passenger car ever built was this Bugatti Royale. It is also called the Golden Bugatti. The car was made in 1931. There were only six Royales made. The car is over 22 feet (6.7 meters) long. The

hood itself is over 7 feet (2 meters) long. The car has an eight-cylinder engine. When it was built, the Royale cost about as much as a large house.

This is a Boeing 747. It is the largest passenger plane. The 747 is made in the United States. But countries all over the world buy and use the 747.

The 747 is 232 feet (70.7 meters) long. Its wingspan is 196 feet (59.7 meters). It can carry up to 500 passengers. The 747 can fly about 6,000 miles (9,650 kilometers) on one load of fuel.

The largest warplane is this
B-52 Stratofortress. It is a bomber
and can carry regular or atomic
bombs. The B-52 is the main
airplane of the Strategic Air
Command (SAC). SAC protects the
United States from air attacks.

The Stratofortress can carry 20 small missiles and a 20,000-pound (9,072-kilogram) bomb load. Its eight jet engines can fly the B-52 for more than 10,000 miles (16,000 kilometers) without refueling.

This is the largest plane ever built. It is the Hercules flying boat, and it is made of plywood. It was designed to carry 700 soldiers. The Hercules cost more than $40 million to build. Its wing span is 320 feet (97.5 meters), which is longer than a football field. In 1947, its eight engines took the Hercules into the air. It flew for about one mile, and then never flew again.

Here is the world's largest
helicopter. It is the Russian Mi-12.
It is also known as ''Homer.'' The
Mi-12 is 121 feet (36.9 meters) long,
and it weighs more than 230,000
pounds (104,325 kilograms). Its
blades span 220 feet (67 meters).
The Mi-12 once carried a load of
more than 88,000 pounds (39,916
kilograms) 7,400 feet (2,255 meters)
into the air.

GLOSSARY

ACV   An aircraft that is held up on a cushion of air. The cushion is formed by the craft's engines. ACV stands for air-cushion-vehicle.

aircraft carrier   A warship that has a deck from which airplanes can take off and land.

bomber   A warplane that carries bombs, which can be dropped on enemy targets.

dragline   A digging machine that works by pulling a large bucket across the ground with strong cables.

dump truck   A truck that carries away ground that has been dug up by earth-moving machines.

earth-moving machine   Any machine that is used to shovel, dig, push, or flatten rocks and soil.

flying boat   An airplane that can land, float, and take off on water.

helicopter   A flying machine that flies by means of long blades that are spun around by an engine on top of the craft.

hovercraft   Another name for an ACV.

passenger ship   A ship that carries people from one place to another.

warplane   An airplane that was made to be used in a war.

warship   A ship that was made to be used in a war.

wingspan   On an airplane, the distance from the tip of one wing to the tip of the other.

INDEX

ACV p. 14
B-52 Stratofortress pp. 24-25
Big Muskie pp. 4-5
Boeing 747 pp. 22-23
Bugatti Royale pp. 20-21
clock pp. 10-11
Double Dude p. 6
dragline p. 5
dump truck pp. 5, 9
Hercules flying boat p. 26
hovercraft pp. 14-15
Mi-12 p. 29
Musashi p. 18
Queen Elizabeth 2 pp. 12-13
SRN-4 p. 15
Titan p. 9
U.S.S. Dwight D. Eisenhower p. 16
U.S.S. New Jersey p. 18-19
U.S.S. Nimitz pp. 16-17
Yamato p. 18